# Garbage and Recycling

by Helen Orme

Consultant: Terry Jennings, Ph.D.
Educational Consultant

## BEARPORT
PUBLISHING

New York, New York

## Credits

Cover and Title Page, © Sam Yeh/AFP/Getty Images and John Solie/Shutterstock; Credit Page, © prism_68/Shutterstock; 4–5, © Camilo Torres/Shutterstock; 6–7, © Stephen Wilkes/Stone/Getty Images; 7, © Kubigula; 8–9, © Peter von Bucher/Shutterstock; 10, © Vyacheslav Osokin/Shutterstock; 11, © Jay S Simon/Stone/Getty Images; 12, © Norman Chan/Shutterstock; 13, © Richard Thornton/Shutterstock; 14–15, © Marcus Clackson/iStockphoto; 16–17, Courtesy of Harold Rushton/www.playmasters.info; 17, © NeonLight/Shutterstock; 18, © Joe Gough/Shutterstock; 18–19, © Eric Gevaert/iStockphoto; 19, © Digital Vision Ltd./SuperStock; 20, © John Glover/Alamy; 21, © Rachel Weill/Jupiterimages; 22–23, © Mark Stout Photography/Shutterstock; 24L, © Kuzma/Shutterstock; 24R, © Lynn Bendickson/Shutterstock; 25, © Condor 36/Shutterstock; 26, © Monkey Business Images/Shutterstock; 27L, © JustASC/Shutterstock; 27R, © sharky/Shutterstock; 28, © Brand X Pictures/Jupiterimages; 29, © Peter Grosch/Shutterstock; 30, © Kenneth V. Pilon/Shutterstock.

Every effort has been made to trace the copyright holders, and we apologize in advance for any unintentional omissions. We would be pleased to insert the appropriate acknowledgments in any subsequent edition of this publication.

The Earth in Danger series is printed on recycled paper.

*Library of Congress Cataloging-in-Publication Data*

Orme, Helen.
    Garbage and recycling / by Helen Orme ; consultant, Terry Jennings.
        p. cm. — (Earth in danger)
    Includes index.
    ISBN-13: 978-1-59716-726-0 (library binding)
    ISBN-10: 1-59716-726-6 (library binding)
    1. Refuse and refuse disposal—Juvenile literature. 2. Recycling (Waste, etc.)—Juvenile literature. I. Jennings, Terry J. II. Title.

    TD792.O76 2008
    363.72'82—dc22

                    2008022361

Copyright © 2008 ticktock Entertainment Ltd.
2 Orchard Business Centre, North Farm Road,
Tunbridge Wells, Kent, TN2 3XF, UK

Published in the United States of America by Bearport Publishing Company, Inc.
United States text copyright © 2009 Bearport Publishing Company, Inc.

For more information, write to Bearport Publishing Company, Inc., 101 Fifth Avenue, Suite 6R, New York, New York 10003. Printed in the United States of America.

10 9 8 7 6 5 4 3 2 1

# Contents

845

# Lots of Garbage

Every day people throw things away—
newspapers, magazines, glass bottles, plastic
containers, metal cans, cardboard boxes, and
leftover food. Even expensive items such as
old or broken computers, cell phones, washing
machines, and cars eventually become garbage.

It might not seem like a person throws out much garbage each day—but it adds up quickly. Each person in the United States throws away an average of about three-quarters of a ton (.68 metric tons) of garbage every year. Where does it all go?

People in the United States throw out more items made from paper than any other kind of material.

**What Do People Throw Away?**

Paper 33.9%

Glass 5.3%

Wood 5.5%

Rubber, Leather, and Textiles 7.3%

Other 3.3%

Yard Trimmings 12.9%

Metals 7.6%

Food Scraps 12.4%

Plastics 11.7%

# Where Does Garbage Go?

Most communities have trucks that pick up garbage. More than half of this garbage is dumped into huge holes in the ground called **landfills**. There, bulldozers flatten the garbage and cover it with a layer of earth. Then more garbage and earth can be put on top of that layer.

As more and more garbage is dumped into a landfill, the landfill gets higher. When the landfill can't hold any more garbage, it is completely covered over with earth. At that point some landfills are turned into parks or parking lots.

*A bulldozer flattening garbage*

*Mount Trashmore Park*

Mount Trashmore Park, in the city of Virginia Beach, Virginia, was once a huge landfill. Today it is a park with playgrounds, a basketball court, hiking trails, picnic areas, two lakes, and a skateboard course.

# The Trouble with Landfills

Turning a landfill into a park sounds like a good idea. Yet landfills create problems.

One problem is that landfills use up a lot of space. Some people don't realize this. They think that garbage in a landfill breaks down and soon turns into soil. That is not what happens, however, to much of the garbage.

Glass cannot break down. Also, many plastics and metals that are put in a landfill today will still be there a thousand years from now. **Biodegradable** materials such as paper can break down, but the process still takes a long time. This is because air helps most materials break down, and little air reaches garbage that is buried underground.

So garbage in a landfill doesn't just disappear. It keeps piling up until there's no room to put in anymore. Then people need a new place to make a new landfill.

About 55 percent of the garbage in the United States is put in landfills. The rest is burned in very large furnaces, called **incinerators**, or **recycled**.

## What Happens to Garbage

Dumped in landfill (55%)

Burned (14%)

Recycled (31%)

# More Landfill Problems

Some of the materials that go into landfills contain dangerous substances, or poisons. For example, batteries, old paint, detergent, plastics, and electronic products such as computers contain substances that can be harmful to people and animals. Rain that falls into landfills mixes with poisons in the garbage.

The poisoned rainwater then seeps deep into the earth, **polluting** both the soil and the water belowground. About 20 percent of our water supply comes from underground. The pollution from landfills can make this water unsafe to drink.

Today, new landfills are lined with plastic and clay. The liners keep landfill poisons out of our water supply. Older landfills, however, are still causing pollution problems.

Some garbage is burned and turned into **ash** before it is placed in a landfill. The ash takes up less space than the garbage. Unfortunately, the smoke from some incinerators pollutes the air with harmful gases.

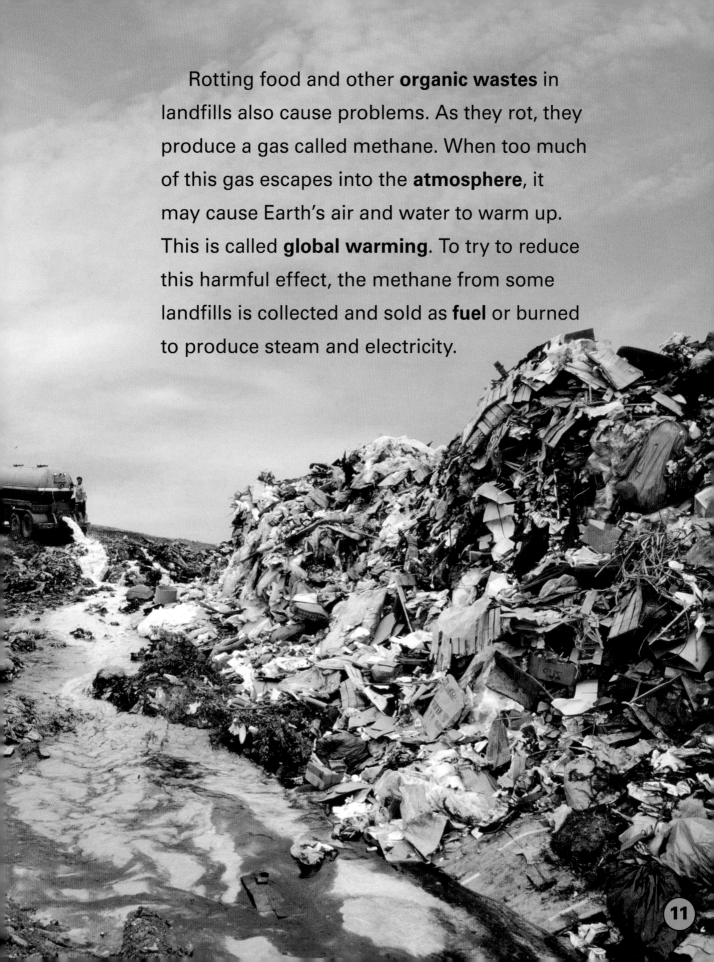

Rotting food and other **organic wastes** in landfills also cause problems. As they rot, they produce a gas called methane. When too much of this gas escapes into the **atmosphere**, it may cause Earth's air and water to warm up. This is called **global warming**. To try to reduce this harmful effect, the methane from some landfills is collected and sold as **fuel** or burned to produce steam and electricity.

# The Recycling Solution

Many of the things people throw away don't actually need to be put in landfills or burned. They can be recycled, instead. When used objects are recycled, they are turned into new objects that people can use. How does garbage get recycled?

*Recycling containers*

People put different kinds of garbage in different recycling containers. For example, objects made out of plastic, metal, glass, and paper are each placed in separate containers. That is because these different materials will be used to make different kinds of things.

Most communities have recycling centers. Trucks may pick up garbage and take it to these centers, or people may take the garbage there themselves. Recycling centers sell garbage to **mills** and factories, where it is made into new things that people can use.

Why is it important to recycle? One reason is that recycled garbage doesn't end up in a landfill or an incinerator. So it doesn't use up land or pollute the air and water. Fortunately, about 65 percent of the garbage people throw away in the United States can be recycled.

*Garbage at a recycling center*

# Recycling Paper

About one-third of people's garbage is paper, and almost all of it can be recycled. At a recycling center, paper is packed into bundles. Then it is sold to a paper mill.

At the mill, the paper is chopped up into little pieces. The chopped-up paper is soaked in water. It turns into a thick mushy liquid called **pulp**. The pulp is treated with chemicals to remove any ink that was on the paper. Sometimes new **wood fiber** is added to the pulp to make it smoother and stronger. Then the pulp is spread out on frames and dried.

The dried pulp is pressed together between heavy rollers to make paper sheets. This recycled paper is sold to companies that make paper towels, toilet paper, napkins, books, paper plates, and other paper products.

*This paper is ready to be recycled.*

Recycling helps protect and save Earth's **natural resources**. For example, in order to make new paper, people need to chop down trees to get wood. Recycled paper, however, is often made from a mixture of recycled and new wood fiber. So fewer trees need to be cut down.

# Recycling Plastic

Much of the food people buy comes in plastic containers. After people eat the food, they often throw away the containers. Yet plastic water bottles, milk jugs, and take-out food containers can often be recycled.

At a recycling center, plastic garbage is cleaned. Then it is sold to factories that turn it into new plastic. The factories first shred or crush the plastic garbage into small pieces. Then the plastic pieces are heated or treated with chemicals, which turn them into a thick, gooey liquid.

This liquid plastic is **molded** to make things such as bottles, playground equipment, tote bags, and outdoor furniture. It can also be spun into **fiber** that is used to make clothing and carpets.

*This playground was made out of recycled plastic.*

New plastic is made from oil. Oil is also used to run cars and machines, as well as heat buildings. Oil comes from the earth. Once all of it is used up, there won't be anymore. So people have to use it carefully. Recycling plastic helps save oil because less oil is needed to make recycled plastic than new plastic.

*Machines pump oil from deep under the ground.*

# Recycling Glass and Metal

Every day, people use glass bottles and jars. Once they are empty, the containers can be recycled to make new ones. At a recycling center, glass bottles and jars are sorted by color. They are then sent to a factory where they are cleaned and crushed. Sand and other materials are added to the broken glass. Then the mixture is melted. Finally, the thick liquid is poured into molds and shaped into new glass bottles and jars.

Many of the foods and liquids people buy come in metal cans. Both aluminum and steel can be recycled.

Old aluminum cans are shredded into small pieces. Then they are melted in a very hot furnace. The hot liquid aluminum is cooled and hardened into huge blocks. Finally, heavy rollers flatten the aluminum blocks into thin sheets. The recycled aluminum is usually made into new cans.

Steel cans are recycled in a similar way. Cars, refrigerators, washing machines, and bridges can all be made out of recycled steel. When they wear out, they can all be recycled again.

In the United States, all steel products are made at least partly with recycled steel. Some steel products are made completely out of recycled steel.

*Steel cans*

# Recycling Organic Waste

Garbage made up of things that were once alive, such as leftover fruits and vegetables, weeds, dead leaves, and grass clippings, is called organic waste. Some people don't throw their organic waste in the garbage. Instead, they recycle it by putting it in a **bin** outdoors. After a while, the waste breaks down into a material that looks like soil. This material is called **compost**.

Compost is used to **fertilize** gardens. It makes flowers and vegetables grow faster. It also makes plants healthier.

*It is much better to use organic waste to help plants grow than to just dump it in a landfill!*

To make compost, put dead leaves, pine needles, grass clippings, and leftover fruits and vegetables into a compost bin. Don't put in any meat, milk, or cheese. Then add some soil, and mix everything together. Every week or so, use a shovel or pitchfork to turn the compost and mix it up. In 10 to 12 weeks, it will be ready to mix into garden soil.

# The Three Rs

Recycling is important. Yet it isn't the only way people can help solve the garbage problem.

People can **reduce** the amount of garbage they create. To do so, they can avoid using **disposable** things, such as paper plates, which get thrown away after one use. They can also try not to buy things that come with a lot of **packaging**. Paper, plastic, and cardboard packaging is usually just thrown away.

Finally, people can **reuse** things. They can either give the things to others or find new uses for the items themselves.

Reduce, reuse, recycle. These are the "three Rs" for solving the garbage problem.

People in the United States throw out 15,000 tons (13,607 metric tons) of packing material each day.

Reusing plastic plates and cups makes less garbage.

## Plastic Bag Problems

Getting rid of plastic bags is a serious garbage problem. Why? Some kinds of plastic bags cannot be recycled. They are often put in landfills, where they can last for more than 1,000 years.

Other plastic bags that aren't thrown in the trash sometimes end up littering streets, getting stuck in trees, or floating in the ocean. They can kill ocean animals that eat them because they mistake the bags for food.

What can people do to help solve the plastic bag problem? They can take their own reusable cloth bags with them when they shop. Then they won't need to use plastic ones.

*Cloth shopping bag*

# Packaging Problems

Much of the food people buy comes in packages. Packaging helps keep food clean and fresh. Yet look at all the packaging that goes into the garbage after one fast-food meal:

| Food Item | Packaging |
|-----------|-----------|
| Hamburger | paper wrapper |
| Ketchup | plastic container |
| French fries | cardboard container |
| Drink | paper cup with a plastic lid |
| Fruit tart | cardboard container |
| Whole meal | paper bag |

*People can reduce the amount of garbage they create by trying not to buy food that comes with a lot of packaging.*

# Just the Facts

## Look for the Symbols

It's important to buy products that can be recycled. It's also important to buy products that are made with recycled materials. Look for these symbols on products or their containers to find out recycling information:

 This symbol means that a product or the container it comes in can be recycled.

 This symbol means that a product is made from recycled materials.

 A percentage number inside a recycling symbol tells how much of the product was made from recycled materials.

# Recycle by Numbers

Different kinds of plastic are used to make different objects. A number appears on the bottom of many plastic containers. That number tells what kind of plastic the container is made of. Here's why it's important to look at the numbers:

- Most recycling centers accept only certain kinds of plastic. Plastics labeled 1 and 2 are the ones most likely to be accepted.

- The number 1 appears on soft drink bottles, water bottles, and peanut butter containers. Number 1 plastic can be used to make tote bags, food containers, and fabric for clothing.

- The number 2 appears on detergent and shampoo bottles, juice bottles, and on yogurt containers. Number 2 plastic can be recycled to make pens, furniture, and fences.

# Reusing

Here are some ways to reuse things instead of throwing them away:

- When you get a gift, save the wrapping paper and reuse it when you have a gift to wrap.

- Use plastic cartons and containers to grow plants in.

- Don't throw away plastic forks and spoons. Wash them so they can be used again.

- Give old clothes to a thrift shop so that other people can use them.

# It's the Law

Some states, cities, and communities in the United States have passed laws to help make sure that people recycle. Here are a few of those laws:

- Newspapers must be made with at least 40 percent recycled paper.

- Stores must take back used cell phones for reuse or recycling with no charge to their customers.

- Stores must offer to sell reusable shopping bags to customers.

- Products that are made out of paper, cardboard, aluminum, glass, or plastic cannot be put in the garbage if they can be recycled.

*Used and broken cell phones*

# How to Help

Everyone needs to get involved to reduce garbage. Here are some things to do:

- Learn as much as possible about recycling. Make a display at school to share what you learned with others.

- Use things longer before throwing them away. For example, if a bicycle breaks, try to get it fixed instead of buying a new one.

- Offer to help your family prepare and take out trash for recycling.

- Encourage your family to use washable cloth napkins and washable plates instead of disposable paper napkins and plates.

- Use things such as paper towel tubes, cardboard boxes, old CDs, and bits of cloth, ribbon, and string to make craft projects.

- Remember the three Rs: Reduce, Reuse, Recycle!

## Learn More Online

To learn more about garbage and recycling, visit
**www.bearportpublishing.com/EarthinDanger**

# Glossary

**ash** (ASH) a powdery substance that is left after something has been burned

**atmosphere** (AT-muhss-fihr) the air, or mixture of gases, that surround Earth

**bin** (BIN) a container for storing things

**biodegradable** (*bye*-oh-di-GRAY-duh-buhl) able to be broken down naturally

**compost** (KOM-pohst) natural material that has rotted and can be added to soil to improve it

**disposable** (diss-POH-zuh-buhl) made to be thrown away after one or several uses

**fertilize** (FUR-tuh-lize) to add material to soil in order to improve the growth of plants

**fiber** (FYE-bur) thread that can be used to make cloth or material

**fuel** (FYOO-uhl) something that is burned to produce heat or power

**global warming** (GLOHB-uhl WORM-ing) the warming of Earth's air and oceans due to a buildup of greenhouse gases in the atmosphere

**incinerators** (in-SIN-uh-*ray*-turz) furnaces for burning garbage

**landfills** (LAND-filz) very large holes in the ground that serve as dumping areas for garbage

**mills** (MILZ) factories that have machinery to process wood, paper, steel, and other materials

**molded** (MOHLD-id) formed into a particular shape by being poured into a container and hardened

**natural resources** (NACH-ur-uhl REE-sorss-iz) materials found in nature, such as trees, water, and coal, that are useful to people

**organic wastes** (or-GAN-ik WAYSTS) garbage that comes from things that were once alive

**packaging** (PAK-ij-ing) wrapping

**polluting** (puh-LOOT-ing) releasing harmful substances into the environment

**pulp** (PUHLP) a soft, wet mixture

**recycled** (ree-SYE-kuhld) when used, old, and unwanted objects are turned into something new and useful

**reduce** (ri-DOOS) to make smaller or less

**reuse** (ree-YOOZ) to use again

**wood fiber** (WUD FYE-bur) small bits of chopped-up wood used to make paper

# Index

# Read More

**Barnham, Kay.** *Recycle (Environment Action!).* New York: Crabtree Publishing Company (2008).

**Fix, Alexandra.** *Glass (Reduce, Reuse, Recycle).* Chicago: Heinemann (2008).

**Walker, Kate.** *Paper (Recycle, Reduce, Reuse, Rethink).* North Mankato, MN: Smart Apple Media (2005).

**Walker, Kate.** *Plastics (Recycle, Reduce, Reuse, Rethink).* North Mankato, MN: Smart Apple Media (2005).